To Jacob & Richard

The Little Book of Teenage - Dad Jokes
101 Nonsense Limericks, Poetry & Verse

by

Sarah Wood

☩ ALETHEIA

Copyright © 2023 Sarah Wood

The right of Sarah Wood to be identified as the author and owner of this Work has been asserted by her in accordance with international copyright precedent and the Berne Convention for the Protection of Literary and Artistic Works (Paris Act, 1971)

All rights reserved. No part of this publication may be reproduced, stored in a retrieval system, or transmitted, in any form or by any means without the prior written permission of the publisher and author, nor be otherwise circulated in any form of binding or cover other than that which it is published and without a similar condition being imposed on the subsequent purchaser.

All characters in this publication are fictitious and any resemblance to real persons, living or dead, is purely coincidental.

A catalogue record for this title is available from the British Library, the United States Library of Congress, and the National Library of New Zealand.

ISBN: *978-1-7395367-0-1*

1st Edition

Printed and bound by Printing Partners, who source FSC-Certified Paper Stock where possible. For Aletheia Press (Liversedge, UK)

CONTENTS

	Acknowledgments	vii
1.	Animals & Pets	1
2.	Christmas Humour	10
3.	Cheeky Children	18
4.	Medical Mishaps	27
5.	Tricky Travel	36
6.	The Not So Natural World	45
7.	Workplace Shenanigans	54
8.	Loopy in Love	63
9.	Suspicious Sport	72
10.	Miscellaneous Mischiefs	79
11.	21st Century Problems	89

ACKNOWLEDGMENTS

With thanks to Richard Wood, Mark Riley, Carrie McKenzie, George Anderson, Jade Scholes, and Dan Raby, for your kind support and artistic donations.

To Mr. Williams, it's not quite the Scottish play and no mockingbirds were killed, but I think you might be slightly proud.

To Clyde, with thanks for your sage advice, fun and creative partnership – Bonnie.

1

ANIMALS & PETS

I went out to buy a carpet
And found a dire little outlet
Which sold shaggy rugs
Where free fleas & bugs
Come into your home at the outset!

There was a man named Doug
Who used to sleep on a rug
One night in such haste
He slept on his face
And now he looks like a Pug!

Imagine a big scary Dragon
Who got pissed drinking out of a flagon
As soon as he cringed
His beard would get singed
Whenever he fell off the wagon!

One day I got a real fright
When my doggy gave me a bite
He chomped my cojones
Right through my pyjamas
I should have turned on the light!

There lives a little doggy down the lane
He comes to me now and again
Every day without fail
He chases his tail
His efforts are always in vain!

Who doesn't love a little pet?
Unless you have to go to the vet
If your cat gets a splinter
It will be a hard winter
Drowning in a mountain of debt!

You could be as dead as a Dodo
Before you are quick to say, 'Oh No!'

Go on, be brisk
And take that risk

Because it's a case of, 'Y.O.L.O'! *

* Street savvy translation – **Y**ou **O**nly **L**ive **O**nce

A keen tofu-muncher from Harrow
Inadvertently swallowed a sparrow
As it flew through her guts
No 'ifs' or 'buts'
It chilled her right through to the marrow!

My cat's name is Pamela
She's known for incredible stamina
When dawdling along
Nothing was wrong
'Til flashed by a yellow speed camera!

2

CHRISTMAS HUMOUR

Christmas Eve at the Dog & Gun
The White Hart, when supping was done
A Quiz at the Sheaf
Last Orders at the Fleece
A Lock-In at the Lion to round off the fun!

Everyone knows good old Santa
But did you know he's allergic to Fanta?
When he drinks just a drop
His bottom goes POP!
And he turns into William Shatner!

I went to the dentists with pain in my teeth
She said, 'Say ah', and looked beneath

My tonsils & tongue

And found something wrong
Some baubles, tinsel, and a Christmas Wreath!

Santa Claus felt a shiver
His lips were all a quiver
He let out a cough
His leg fell off
And floated down the river!

We all love a festive Farm Shop
Pigs in blankets & Barnsley Chop
Christmas cake & coffee
A selection of toffee
All wrapped up, & ready to Pop!

My Christmas wish is World Peace
That moment when all wars cease
It should have happened by now
If we'd worked out how
We should question what lies beneath...

On Christmas Eve with a drunken wobble
I twisted my foot on a cobble
It supported my goal
To claim on the dole
I walk everywhere now with a hobble!

When you're hanging your Christmas lights
Don't get into a festive fight
Make sure you are kind
Or you will be confined
To spend the rest of your day up tight!

3

CHEEKY CHILDREN

There was a kid called Kane
Who struggled a bit with his aim
When he went for a poo
And missed the loo
His street-cred was never the same!

There was a cute girl of four
Who was always asking for MORE!
One day she said, 'Mummy
give me more for my tummy.
Or I'll kick an scream on the floor!'

Why do kids have to yell?
When it's easier simply to 'tell'
They're so bloody noisy
It really annoys me
And could wake up the Devil in hell!

I picked up my child from school
But he no longer thinks I'm 'cool'

Now I must wait

10 Yards from the gate
Apparently, that's the new rule!

I hate changing a nappy!
Especially when it's quite crappy

The Human 'goo'

Which is made out of poo
Does not make me feel very happy!

Not everyone likes going to school
Here is the critical rule
Go every day
And soon it will pay
You won't end up broke like a fool!

I do love a nice cup of tea
I think most kids would agree
It should be made in a pot
'Cause if it is not
Then grandma gets angry with me!

Before you get into your Car
Especially when travelling far

Here is my plea

Take your kids for a pee
Or they'll have to wee in a jar!

There was a toddler named Beryl
Who was born & raised on the Wirral
Her house was a lair
She had untidy hair
One might describe her as feral!

4

MEDICAL MISHAPS

A man poked out his eyeball
Which led to a dangerous fall
His body went stiff
As he fell off a cliff
Now he is DEAD, that is all!

There once was a female nurse
Who liked to keep rats in her purse
One day whilst at work
They all went berserk
And she ended up in a hearse!

A poor young lady called Clare
Ran over hot coals as a dare
But she tripped on her gown
Which made her fall down
And promptly set fire to her hair!

Don't stand too close to a Pylon
Especially when wearing nylon
If you touch the wrong wire
You might expire
Or melt some parts you rely on!

I once met a guy called Si
He went for an MRI
Be careful, they said
If there's metal in your head
It will launch you into the sky!

Here is a tale of Dos Amigos
One of whom had gangrenous toes
He said to the other
'Hey there Brother!'
When they drop off, I'll nick some of yours!

There once was a bloke called Keith
He didn't have any teeth
Targeting pensioners
He stole their dentures
Now he's a known dental thief!

There was an Egyptian mummy
He went to the beach, it was sunny
And whilst he napped
He completely unwrapped
Now he's all soft and runny!

I went on a day trip to York
To purchase a whole side of Pork
It was a bridge too far
To lift into my car
And now I'm unable to walk!

5

TRICKY TRAVEL

A lady was once stuck in traffic
Whilst driving her automatic
Throughout the ordeal
She lost a wheel
And now she's totally static!

We buy cars for cash
Motors that have been in a bash
We Cut & Shut
And polish them up, then
We take your money and dash!

There's a part that's hard to reach
It's a skill that's hard to teach
When you can't get to your crack
Or the small of your back
With the suntan cream on the beach!

I have an electric car
And I never get very far
I go to the pub
With a charging hub
Then I can't escape from the bar!

There's a couple called Sarah & Rich
Their limericks they would pitch
Whilst they were driving
Ideas were thriving
Let's hope they don't crash in a ditch!

I wanted some nifty new wheels
Shopped around to get some good deals
Although it looks great
With the latest plate
Turning right, the bloody thing squeals!

When the traffic lights are red
And the gridlock stops you dead
With potholes galore
Roadworks and more
You might as well stay in your bed!

One day whilst flying off the coast
One engine was suddenly toast

I kept myself sane

An inverted the plane
Then landed with grace utmost!

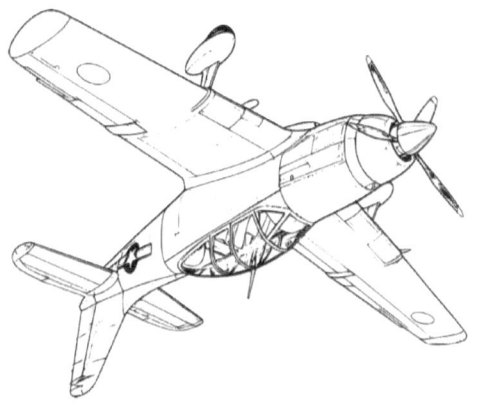

I hate it when drivers push in
I see it as a cardinal sin
With no indicator
They say, 'See you later!'
Let's chuck them all in the bin!

6

THE NOT SO NATURAL WORLD

There once was a man called Lee
Who looked a bit like a tree
But soon his green thumb
Would sprout out his bum
Whenever he went for a wee!

There was a forgetful farmer
Who wanted to be much warmer
So he put on his coat
An inside found a note
Don't forget to light the wood burner!

Consider for a moment, the Sun
He's lonely without any fun
When the moon leaves the sky
She's like, 'Sorry, gotta fly!'
Of course, a new day has begun!

I'm just a little bananas
I like to cause lots of dramas
I won't go to bed
Go cow tipping instead
To piss off all of the farmers!

When out an about in the fog
I don't recommend that you jog
One foot out of place
You'll be out of the race
Lying face down in a bog!

I signed up to 'Yorkshire in Bloom'
But experienced a sense of doom

It was such a blow

When nothing would grow
Apart from a magic mushroom!

A red sky in the morning
It's said is a 'Shepherd's Warning'
But the Shepherd's in bed
'Cause his Collie dropped dead
And all his Sheep are still yawning!

It's hard being Jack Frost
It comes at personal cost
Amongst all the ice
He's let go of what's nice
His pale blue heart is quite lost!

I drive to work in the morning
And see the new day dawning
'I'm so tired', I said
'Can I go back to bed?
I can't stop myself yawning!'

7

WORKPLACE SHENANIGANS

Consider the Workplace 'bubble'
Which can easily land you in trouble
'Cc' the wrong Jim
Whilst complaining to Kim
You'll get your P45 on the double!

There was a bloke called Norman
Who used to work as a Doorman

He got into a fight
But then, 'Saw the Light'
Now he's a practising Mormon!

A baker was baking some bread
Some dough entered into his head
It got in through his nose
An when the dough rose
'I look like Frank Sidebottom!', he said!

Let's celebrate the mighty bin man!
Riding like Kings on a Tip Van
Moving with haste
Through Toxic Waste
With skin like leather and perma-tan!

NEVER mess with the Undertaker
He's actually a bit of a ball-breaker
He's best friends with Death
Who'll extinguish your breath
Then send you to meet your maker!

A farmhand once stole a tractor
Stating mental health was a factor
But the farmer, in time
Found her bragging online
It was all B.S, so he sacked her!

Who would trust a politician?
They're full of dodgy information
They're never on the level
Sell their souls to the devil
In exchange for power of the nation!

It's all just a matter of class
Said the Navy's very top brass
If you join the army
You're totally barmy
You'll find yourself pushing up grass!

Always put knickers in the wash-bin
Make sure you NEVER leave them in
The leg of your trousers
Then walk out your houses
When they drop out it is embarrassing!

8

LOOPY IN LOVE

Every good boy goes to Church
So upon the pews I would perch
But I'm too easily led
Worship women instead
And leave poor old God in the lurch!

I once was married to a spy
To whom I could never lie
It wasn't the look on my face
That gave me away
But the polygraph machine in his tie!

There was a girl looking for love
Who prayed to the God above
'Please bring me a boy,
Go on don't be coy
Please give cupid a shove!'

Never fall in love with a builder
Was the lesson learned by Hilda
When she answered her door
She fell through the floor
Her husband damn nearly killed her!

One day you will find your soulmate
It's simply a matter of fate
Just login online
And type, 'Free 69'
It will drastically shorten your wait!

King Henry the VIII was a nutter
Going through wives like
A knife through butter
One morning he said
'Off with her head!'
Then off she would go to the Cutter!

I've got a wonderful life
Alongside the 'trouble and strife'
She loves the 'old pot and pan'
She says I'm "Her man"
Thank God I made her my wife!

The curious tale of Medusa
No man could ever seduce her
With snakes in her hair
And a steely cold stare
To stone, she will reduce ya!

Ya' gotta love a rough & ready tart
Especially when she lets out a fart
Lipstick on her teeth
And a boyfriend called Keith
This kind of chav is an art!

9

SUSPICIOUS SPORT

I once went Scuba Diving
To find out the fishes were thriving!
The Salmon kept pace
And so did the Plaice
And the John Dories were jiving!

Curling is a curious sport
It takes a particular sort
Who sweep like crazy
The opposite of lazy
In fact, 'Pro-Cleaners' on an ice-court!

The dangerous sport of Fencing
Involves a lot of arse clenching

In one split sec

An a foil through your neck
Your buttocks will cease from tensing!

A skydiver believed he could fly
He was a very arrogant guy
He jumped out of his flat
And promptly went splat!
Turns out it was 'Pie in the Sky'!

A sign said, 'Keep to your Lanes'
But one would have been at pains
To stick to that pact
When in actual fact
The lane divider was all that remained!

'Three strikes and you're out!'
The Umpire said, 'There's
no use messing about!
If you're going to play dirty
I'll have to get 'Shirty'
And then I'll give you a clout!'

The Swimmer's golden perma-tan
Hid where her legs ended & began
Though she had pouty red lips
And wiggled her hips
It was clear she was really a man!

10

MISCELLANEOUS MISCHIEFS

How to annoy all of your friends?
Should you want to? That depends
You could dish out a medley
Of Silent but Deadly
That's where your friendship ends!

It is quite a chore going to bed
When you've horns growing out of your head
'I wake up dishevelled'
Complained the Devil
'No wonder my face is all red!'

A man put his stuff in self-storage
So he could stop paying his mortgage
He stored one thousand Beer Cans
And both of his Grans
The company charged him corkage!

If by some unfortunate chance
A serial killer asks you to dance

Spin him around

'Til his feet leave the ground
Then tie him up with his pants!

Discover the real value of gold
Precious? To have and to hold
Remember poor Gollum?
It made him quite solemn
That story never gets told!

A girl who lived for her diet
Could never keep her gut quiet
She ate less and less
And so, in protest
Her intestines started to riot!

There once was a lady called Kath
Who spent too much time in the bath
She soaked until noon
'Til she looked like a prune
Then got out, an made everyone laugh!

Satan is a lazy bastard!
Who spends half his life plastered
He lives in his shed
Spends all day in bed
I'm surprised at how long he's lasted!

There once was a good guitarist
Who said, 'Writing songs is the hardest'
He started to sing
Then Ping! Went a string
It happens to all the top artists!

In the beautiful morning sunrise
Yawn, stretch & open your eyes
Get out of your pit
You lazy shit
This is where the fairy-tale dies!

11

21ST CENTURY PROBLEMS

Round up the actors in Hollywood
Losing those who are no good
Including the 'woke'
And the ones who are broke
You'll have a Christian brotherhood!

There once was a lady named Mary
Her behaviour was quite contrary
Her husband did sulk
When he said, 'Pass the milk'
She said, 'I can't, I'm allergic to dairy!'

I'll tell you a tale about 'Dark' & 'Light'
A time they got into a little fight
They were having a natter
Concerning 'Dark Matter'
Each of them thought they were right!

I once took a trip to Texaco
But found the petrol was very low
They said, 'On 'yer bike
Saudi's on strike
The last delivery was weeks ago!'

People think I'm a geek
Here's what I do every week
90 hours on my phone
Playing games all alone
I'm a complete digital freak!

Do you have a 'Can Do' attitude?
Do you live your life 'In Gratitude'?
No! It's all just a farce
Shove your morals up your arse!
We don't need another fucking platitude!

Smart criminals are VERY rare
Most of them just don't care
They don't give a fuck
When the game is up
Just give you the thousand yard stare!

You're not moving out when you're 18
You are being just a little keen
The whole bloody nation
Suffers crippling inflation
Thoughts of independence are a dream!

I decided to try out fasting
But I can't really see it lasting

My poor old gut

Thinks my throat's been cut
And all I want is a pasty!

Big brother's got his eye on you...
Never off duty - even in the loo!
'Shit stats' are a measure
At his majesty's pleasure
It's over when they're counting poo!

The problem of energy without coal
Is a bit like rice crispies in a bowl
Only takes a cold SNAP
And the demand will CRACK
And POP 'renewables' as a whole!

I bought a nice house with a view
And this was the council's queue
To grant planning permission
For a Barratt Homes 'vision'
All I see is the neighbour's loo!

Every night I have the same dream
I'm stuck in an online 'meme'
On my forehead a note
Or a smug little quote
And some 'Woke' pop-culture scene!

ABOUT THE AUTHOR

Sarah is an engineer who lives in Yorkshire with her husband and son, having a creative mid-life crisis after 20 years of logic.

Alliance of Independent Authors

www.ingramcontent.com/pod-product-compliance
Lightning Source LLC
LaVergne TN
LVHW091601060526
838200LV00036B/946